# SONS OF THE LAND
## Transatlantic Slave Trade And
## The Chinese Neocolonialism

### Sheriff Olagboye

# TABLE OF CONTENT

INTRODUCTION

CHAPTER ONE

CHAPTER TWO

CHAPTER THREE

CHAPTER FOUR

CHAPTER FIVE

CHAPTER SIX

CHAPTER SEVEN

CHAPTER EIGHT

# INTRODUCTION

The history of human civilization is marked by the exploitation of one group by another, and the transatlantic slave trade and Chinese neocolonialism are two of the most prominent examples of this phenomenon. These events had far-reaching and profound impacts on the world, shaping its political, economic, and social structures in ways that still resonate today.

Sons of the Land: Transatlantic Slave Trade and the Chinese Neocolonialism is a comprehensive examination of these two events and their impact on the world. Through in-depth research and analysis, this book explores the historical, economic, political, and social forces that drove the transatlantic slave trade and Chinese neocolonialism, and the devastating consequences that they had for the peoples and nations affected by them.

This book is a powerful call to action, urging us to learn from the mistakes of the past and work to create a more equitable and sustainable world. It makes the case that the legacy of the transatlantic slave trade and Chinese neocolonialism is not only a matter of history, but a matter of current and future concern, as the forces that drove these events continue to shape the world today.

This book is an essential resource for anyone interested in understanding the impact of the transatlantic slave trade and Chinese neocolonialism, and for anyone seeking to promote a more just and equitable world. It is a compelling and persuasive work that will challenge your assumptions and deepen your understanding of these critical issues. So come and embark on a journey with us, as we explore the complexities of the transatlantic slave trade and the rise of Chinese neocolonialism.

# CHAPTER ONE

## Introduction to Transatlantic Slave Trade

The transatlantic slave trade, also known as the Middle Passage, was one of the largest forced migrations in human history. Over a period of nearly four centuries, millions of Africans were forcibly taken from their homes and transported across the Atlantic Ocean to the Americas to work as enslaved labor on plantations, mines, and in households. The transatlantic slave trade was a brutal and inhumane system that had far-reaching and long-lasting consequences on the African continent and the African diaspora.

## Historical background and causes of the slave trade

The transatlantic slave trade began in the late 15th century and continued until the 19th century. The demand for enslaved labor was driven by the growth of European colonial empires in the Americas, as well as by the need for labor to work on sugar, tobacco, and cotton plantations. European slave traders formed alliances with African rulers, who sold prisoners of war, criminals, and debtors as slaves in exchange for goods such as guns, textiles, and metal goods.

The transatlantic slave trade was fueled by the economic, political, and ideological interests of European powers. The slave trade was a profitable and profitable venture for European slave traders and plantation owners, and it was supported by the Catholic Church and European governments. European slave traders also used racial ideologies to justify the enslavement of Africans, claiming that Africans were inferior and uncivilized, and that enslavement was a way to "civilize" them.

## The impact of the transatlantic slave trade

The transatlantic slave trade had a profound impact on Africa and the Americas. On the African continent, the slave trade disrupted local economies and societies, as enslaved Africans were taken from their homes and families and their communities were left without their labor and expertise. The slave trade also led to the loss of human capital, as millions of the most skilled and talented Africans were taken to the Americas, leaving a lasting impact on the African continent.

In the Americas, the transatlantic slave trade was the cornerstone of the slave-based economy that powered the growth of the colonial empires and the formation of the modern world. Enslaved Africans worked in brutal and inhumane conditions, building the wealth and power of the European colonies and their ruling classes. The legacy of slavery continues to shape the social, political, and economic structures of the Americas, and its effects are still felt today in the form of institutionalized racism and discrimination.

In conclusion, the transatlantic slave trade was a brutal and inhumane system that had far-reaching and long-lasting consequences on the African continent and the African diaspora. Understanding the historical background, causes, and impact of the transatlantic slave trade is essential for understanding the legacy of slavery and its continued impact on the world today.

# CHAPTER TWO

## The Middle Passage and the Life of Enslaved Africans

The transatlantic slave trade was a traumatic and brutal experience for the millions of enslaved Africans who were forcibly taken from their homes and transported across the Atlantic Ocean to the Americas. The journey across the Atlantic, known as the Middle Passage, was a horrific experience that took a heavy toll on the physical and mental well-being of enslaved Africans.

## The journey across the Atlantic

The journey across the Atlantic was a long and dangerous one, lasting anywhere from several weeks to several months. Enslaved Africans were packed into ships like cargo, often in cramped and unsanitary conditions, with limited access to food, water, and fresh air. The Middle Passage was a time of extreme suffering for enslaved Africans, as they were subjected to disease, starvation, and physical abuse by the crew of the ship.

Many enslaved Africans did not survive the journey, and their bodies were thrown overboard into the ocean. The journey across the Atlantic was a traumatic and life-altering experience for the enslaved Africans who survived, and it marked the beginning of a life of exploitation and oppression in the Americas.

**Living conditions of enslaved Africans in the Americas**

Enslaved Africans who survived the Middle Passage faced a life of exploitation and oppression in the Americas. They were forced to work long hours in brutal conditions on plantations, mines, and in households, often without adequate food, clothing, or shelter. Enslaved Africans were subjected to physical abuse, including whippings, beatings, and other forms of punishment, and they were denied basic human rights and freedoms.

Enslaved Africans were also subjected to cultural and psychological violence, as their African cultural and spiritual practices were suppressed, and they were forced to adopt the beliefs and customs of their enslavers. This was an attempt by slave owners to control the minds and spirits of enslaved Africans, and to make them more compliant and obedient.

## Resistance and rebellion against slavery

Despite the brutal conditions of slavery, enslaved Africans resisted their exploitation and oppression in various ways. Some enslaved Africans rebelled against their enslavement by staging armed uprisings and rebellions, while others engaged in passive resistance, such as sabotaging plantation equipment, slowing their work pace, or engaging in work slowdowns.

Enslaved Africans also created their own cultures, communities, and religious practices, as a way to resist cultural suppression and to preserve their African heritage. They also used their music, dance, and storytelling to resist their enslavement, and to communicate their experiences and struggles to each other and future generations.

In conclusion, the Middle Passage and life of enslaved Africans was a time of extreme suffering and exploitation. Despite the brutal conditions of slavery, enslaved Africans resisted their enslavement in various ways, and they created their own cultures, communities, and religious practices as a way to resist oppression and to preserve their African heritage. Understanding the experiences of enslaved Africans is essential for understanding the legacy of slavery and its continued impact on the African diaspora today.

# CHAPTER THREE

## The Abolition Movement and the End of Slavery

The transatlantic slave trade was a brutal and inhumane practice that lasted for centuries. However, the abolition movement, a global movement aimed at ending slavery, eventually brought an end to the transatlantic slave trade and slavery itself. This chapter will explore the origins and development of the abolition movement, and its ultimate success in ending slavery.

## Origins of the Abolition Movement

The abolition movement has its roots in the late 18th and early 19th centuries, when European and American intellectuals, religious leaders, and political activists began to question the morality and legality of slavery. Some of these early abolitionists were motivated by religious beliefs, such as the belief in the equality of all human beings and the idea that slavery was a sin. Others were motivated by political or economic ideals, such as the belief in the importance of individual freedom and the idea that slavery was an inefficient and unjust system of labor.

## The Abolition Movement in Europe and America

The abolition movement gained momentum in Europe and America in the late 18th and early 19th centuries, as more and more people joined the cause. Abolitionist societies and organizations were formed, and influential figures such as William Wilberforce in Britain and Abraham Lincoln in America emerged as leaders of the movement.

Abolitionist societies and organizations conducted public campaigns, publishing anti-slavery literature, organizing public demonstrations, and staging political actions. They also advocated for the abolition of slavery through the legal system, by filing lawsuits and lobbying for legislative change.

## The Abolition of Slavery

The abolition movement eventually succeeded in bringing an end to the transatlantic slave trade and slavery itself. Britain was the first major nation to abolish the transatlantic slave trade in 1807, and other nations soon followed suit. The United States abolished slavery in 1865, following the Civil War, and slavery was eventually abolished throughout the Americas in the late 19th and early 20th centuries.

The abolition of slavery was a major turning point in world history, and it marked the end of one of the most brutal and inhumane practices in human history. However, the legacy of slavery and the abolition movement continues to shape the world today, as the descendants of enslaved Africans continue to face the legacy of slavery, including systemic discrimination and economic inequality.

In conclusion, the abolition movement was a global movement that brought an end to the transatlantic slave trade and slavery itself. The movement was driven by a diverse range of motivations, including religious, political, and economic ideals, and it was successful in bringing about legislative change and the eventual abolition of slavery. Understanding the abolition movement and its legacy is essential for understanding the impact of slavery on the world today.

# CHAPTER FOUR

## The Legacy of Slavery and the Impact on Modern Society

The transatlantic slave trade and slavery had a profound and lasting impact on the world, shaping the course of history and affecting the lives of millions of people for centuries. In this chapter, we will explore the legacy of slavery and its impact on modern society.

## Economic and Social Inequality

One of the most profound impacts of slavery was the creation of economic and social inequality. Enslaved Africans were forced to work without pay and were denied the basic rights and freedoms that other people enjoyed. This created a deep divide between the descendants of enslaved

Africans and other groups, which has persisted to the present day.

In many countries, including the United States, the descendants of enslaved Africans continue to face significant economic and social disadvantages, including poverty, unemployment, and discrimination. These disparities have been perpetuated by a range of systemic and institutional factors, including the legacy of slavery, ongoing discrimination, and the lack of investment in communities of color.

## Cultural and Political Legacy

The legacy of slavery also extends to the cultural and political spheres, affecting the way that people think and act, and shaping the political discourse and policies of nations. Slavery has left a lasting impact on the cultural identity of African Americans, and it has influenced the way that people understand and interpret history, culture, and politics.

Slavery has also had a lasting impact on the political landscape of many countries, shaping the political discourse and policies of nations, and influencing the way that people understand and participate in the political process. For example, slavery played a major role in the formation of the United States and continues to shape the political discourse and policies of the nation today.

In conclusion, the legacy of slavery and the impact of slavery on modern society are profound and far-reaching. The legacy of slavery has perpetuated economic and social inequality, shaped cultural and political identity, and influenced the political discourse and policies of nations. Understanding the legacy of slavery and its impact on modern society is essential for understanding the world today and working to create a more just and equal society.

Continuing from the previous content, it is important to recognize that the legacy of slavery has also had a global impact, affecting not just the countries that were involved in the transatlantic slave trade but also the entire world. Slavery has contributed to global inequalities and has shaped the economic, political, and cultural landscape of many countries, influencing the way that people think, act, and interact with one another.

For example, the slave trade and slavery contributed to the development of capitalism and the global economy, as the profits from slavery helped to finance industrialization and the growth of commerce and trade. The legacy of slavery has also shaped the political landscape of many countries, influencing the development of democracies and the institutions of the modern state.

The legacy of slavery has also had a profound impact on the way that people understand and relate to one another. Slavery has contributed to the creation of racial and ethnic categories, and has influenced the way that people think about race, ethnicity, and cultural identity. Slavery has also contributed to the development of discriminatory attitudes and practices, perpetuating inequality and division in many countries.

In conclusion, the legacy of slavery is complex and far-reaching, affecting not just the countries involved in the transatlantic slave trade but also the entire world. The legacy of slavery has perpetuated economic and social inequality, shaped cultural and political identity, and influenced the political discourse and policies of nations. Understanding the legacy of slavery and its impact on the world is essential for working to create a more just and equal society and for building a more peaceful and prosperous future.

# CHAPTER FIVE

## The Fight Against Slavery and the Path to Reparations

The transatlantic slave trade and slavery were among the most shameful and unjust practices in human history, and for centuries, people have been fighting to end slavery and to seek justice for the victims of slavery. In this chapter, we will explore the fight against slavery and the path to reparations for the victims of slavery.

## The Abolitionist Movement

The fight against slavery began long before the formal abolition of slavery in many countries. In the late 18th and early 19th centuries, a movement of abolitionists emerged in Europe and North America, who advocated for the end of slavery and the rights of enslaved Africans. These abolitionists were a diverse group of people, including religious leaders, politicians, and activists, who used a range of tactics, including protest, petition, and litigation, to call for an end to slavery.

In the United States, the abolitionist movement was led by figures such as Frederick Douglass and Harriet Tubman, who escaped slavery and became prominent voices in the fight against slavery. The abolitionist movement played a key role in bringing the issue of slavery to the forefront of the public debate, and helped to build momentum for the formal abolition of slavery in many countries.

**The Formal Abolition of Slavery**

The formal abolition of slavery was a slow and difficult process, and in many countries, it took many years of struggle and advocacy before slavery was finally abolished. In the United States, for example, slavery was not formally abolished until the passage of the 13th Amendment to the Constitution in 1865, following the end of the Civil War.

In other countries, such as the British Empire, slavery was gradually abolished through a series of laws and reforms, and in many other countries, slavery was abolished as a result of political revolutions and upheavals.

## The Path to Reparations

The fight for justice for the victims of slavery has continued long after the formal abolition of slavery, as people have sought reparations for the harm and injustices inflicted by slavery. The demand for reparations has been driven by the descendants of enslaved Africans, who have argued that slavery and its aftermath have left a lasting impact on their communities, perpetuating economic and social inequalities and perpetuating discrimination and injustice.

The demand for reparations has taken many forms, including calls for financial compensation, apologies, and the recognition of the harm and injustices inflicted by slavery. In recent years, there has been growing momentum for reparations, with many countries and organizations acknowledging the need for reparations and taking steps to address the legacy of slavery.

In conclusion, the fight against slavery and the path to reparations for the victims of slavery is an ongoing and important struggle, and it is a testament to the resilience and determination of people who have fought for justice and equality throughout history. Understanding the fight against slavery and the path to reparations is essential for building a more just and equal world, and for ensuring that the legacy of slavery is never forgotten.

# CHAPTER SIX

## The Legacy of Slavery in the Modern World

The legacy of slavery continues to shape the world in profound and far-reaching ways, and in this chapter, we will explore the ongoing impact of slavery on modern society.

## Economic Inequality

The legacy of slavery has had a significant impact on economic inequality, both within countries and globally. Slavery has contributed to the concentration of wealth and power in the hands of a few, and has perpetuated economic inequalities and disparities, particularly for African descendants and other people of color.

For example, slavery and its aftermath have contributed to the underdevelopment of many African countries and communities, perpetuating poverty and inequality and limiting access to opportunities and resources. In the United States and other countries, slavery has contributed to persistent racial wealth and income disparities, with people of color facing significant obstacles in building wealth and achieving economic stability.

## Discrimination and Injustice

The legacy of slavery has also contributed to ongoing discrimination and injustice, perpetuating inequality and division in many societies. Slavery has contributed to the development of discriminatory attitudes and practices, and has influenced the way that people think about race, ethnicity, and cultural identity.

For example, slavery has contributed to the criminalization of people of color and has perpetuated the use of mass incarceration as a tool of social control, leading to significant racial disparities in the criminal justice system. Slavery has also contributed to ongoing discrimination in housing, education, and the workplace, perpetuating inequality and limiting access to opportunities and resources.

## Cultural and Political Identity

The legacy of slavery has also shaped cultural and political identity, influencing the way that people understand and relate to one another. Slavery has contributed to the creation of racial and ethnic categories, and has influenced the way that people think about race, ethnicity, and cultural identity.

For example, slavery has contributed to the development of a racialized political discourse and has shaped the political landscape of many countries, influencing the development of democracies and the institutions of the modern state. Slavery has also influenced the way that people think about cultural identity, influencing the development of cultural movements and shaping the way that people understand and express their cultural heritage.

In conclusion, the legacy of slavery continues to shape the modern world in profound and far-reaching ways, perpetuating economic inequality, discrimination and injustice, and shaping cultural and political identity. Understanding the legacy of slavery and its impact on the world is essential for working to create a more just and equal society and for building a more peaceful and prosperous future.

# CHAPTER SEVEN

**The Rise of Chinese Neocolonialism**

In recent decades, China has emerged as a major economic and political power, and its influence has been felt around the world, particularly in the developing world. In this chapter, we will explore the rise of Chinese neocolonialism and its impact on the global economy and politics.

**Economic Dominance**

China has become a major economic power in recent decades, and its influence is being felt around the world. China has become a major source of investment and trade for many countries, and its economic dominance has led to the development of new economic relationships and dependencies.

For example, many countries in Africa and other developing regions have become heavily dependent on China for trade and investment, and China has become a major player in the global commodity markets, exerting significant control over the prices of key commodities. China's economic dominance has also led to the creation of new trade and investment arrangements, such as the Belt and Road Initiative, which has the potential to reshape the global economy.

## Political Influence

In addition to its economic dominance, China has also emerged as a major political power, and its influence has been felt in many countries around the world. China has used its economic power to build political alliances, to shape the development of international institutions, and to advance its own political interests.

For example, China has used its economic influence to build political alliances with countries in the developing world, particularly in Africa, and has used its economic power to advance its own political interests in the region. China has also become a major player in international institutions, such as the United Nations, and has used its influence to shape the development of these institutions in ways that support its own interests.

## The Rise of Neocolonialism

The rise of Chinese neocolonialism has significant implications for the global economy and politics, and raises important questions about the future of the world order. China's economic dominance and political influence have led to the creation of new economic relationships and dependencies, and have the potential to reshape the global economy and the balance of power in the world.

For example, the rise of Chinese neocolonialism raises important questions about the future of the global trading system, and the role of international institutions in promoting economic growth and stability. It also raises important questions about the future of democracy and human rights, and the extent to which countries in the developing world will be able to resist Chinese influence and maintain their independence.

The rise of Chinese neocolonialism represents a major shift in the global economy and politics, and has significant implications for the future of the world order. Understanding the rise of Chinese neocolonialism and its impact on the global economy and politics is essential for working to create a more just and equitable world and for building a more prosperous and peaceful future.

It is also important to note that the rise of Chinese neocolonialism has been met with resistance from some countries and communities who are concerned about the impact of Chinese economic and political influence on their independence and sovereignty. There have been widespread concerns about the terms of Chinese investment and trade deals, particularly with regards to the exploitation of natural resources and the exploitation of labor.

In many countries, there have been protests against Chinese investment projects and trade deals, and there has been growing criticism of the human rights abuses associated with Chinese investment and trade. The impact of Chinese neocolonialism has also been felt in the global political arena, where there has been increasing criticism of China's role in international institutions and its use of its economic power to advance its political interests.

It is clear that the rise of Chinese neocolonialism represents a major challenge for the global community, and that addressing its impact will require a coordinated response from governments, civil society organizations, and the international community more broadly. This will require a greater understanding of the complexities of Chinese neocolonialism, and a commitment to promoting more equitable and sustainable economic relationships between China and the developing world.

In conclusion, chapter 7 highlights the rise of Chinese neocolonialism and its impact on the global economy and politics. It is important to understand the complexities of Chinese neocolonialism and to work towards a more equitable and sustainable world that promotes the interests of all nations and communities.

# CHAPTER EIGHT

## The Consequences of Chinese Neocolonialism

The rise of Chinese neocolonialism has significant consequences for the global economy and politics, and has the potential to reshape the world in profound ways. In this chapter, we will explore the consequences of Chinese neocolonialism and their impact on the developing world, the global economy, and the future of the world order.

### Impact on the Developing World

One of the most significant consequences of Chinese neocolonialism is its impact on the developing world. Many countries in the developing world have become heavily dependent on China for trade and investment, and China's economic dominance has led to the development of new economic relationships and dependencies.

For example, the impact of Chinese neocolonialism has been felt in Africa, where many countries have become heavily dependent on China for trade and investment. This has led to the exploitation of natural resources, the exploitation of labor, and the growth of corruption and illicit financial flows. In addition, China's political influence has led to the erosion of democracy and human rights in many countries in the developing world, as China has used its economic power to advance its own political interests in the region.

## Impact on the Global Economy

Another significant consequence of Chinese neocolonialism is its impact on the global economy. China's economic dominance has led to the creation of new economic relationships and dependencies, and has the potential to reshape the global economy in profound ways.

For example, the rise of Chinese neocolonialism has led to the creation of new trade and investment arrangements, such as the Belt and Road Initiative, which has the potential to reshape the global economy. This has led to concerns about the future of the global trading system and the role of international institutions in promoting economic growth and stability. In addition, China's economic dominance has led to the creation of new economic dependencies, which has the potential to exacerbate global economic imbalances and increase economic instability.

## Impact on the Future of the World Order

The rise of Chinese neocolonialism has significant implications for the future of the world order, and raises important questions about the balance of power in the world.

China's economic dominance and political influence have led to the creation of new economic relationships and dependencies, and have the potential to reshape the global economy and the balance of power in the world.

For example, the rise of Chinese neocolonialism raises important questions about the future of democracy and human rights, and the extent to which countries in the developing world will be able to resist Chinese influence and maintain their independence. It also raises important questions about the future of the global trading system, and the role of international institutions in promoting economic growth and stability.

In conclusion, the consequences of Chinese neocolonialism are significant, and have the potential to reshape the world in profound ways. Understanding the consequences of Chinese neocolonialism and their impact on the developing world, the global economy, and the future of the world order is essential for working to create a more just and equitable world and for building a more prosperous and peaceful future.

Furthermore, the rise of Chinese neocolonialism also has implications for global security, as it raises questions about the distribution of military power and the stability of the global security system. China's growing military and political influence has led to concerns about its intentions and the potential for conflict, and has led to the development of new security arrangements, such as the Quadrilateral Security Dialogue between the United States, India, Japan, and Australia.

Moreover, the rise of Chinese neocolonialism has also raised questions about the role of the United States and other Western powers in the world, and their ability to maintain their influence in the face of growing Chinese power. There has been growing concern about the decline of American power and influence, and the need for a more coordinated and effective response from the international community to address the rise of Chinese neocolonialism.

In response to the rise of Chinese neocolonialism, there have been calls for a more equitable and sustainable world order, one that promotes the interests of all nations and communities, and that works to promote economic growth, stability, and security for all. This will require a greater understanding of the complexities of Chinese neocolonialism, and a commitment to promoting more equitable and sustainable economic relationships between China and the developing world.

In conclusion, the rise of Chinese neocolonialism has significant implications for the global economy, politics, security, and the future of the world order, and addressing its impact will require a coordinated response from governments, civil society organizations, and the international community more broadly. By working together, we can build a more equitable and sustainable world, and ensure a more prosperous and peaceful future for all.

www.ingramcontent.com/pod-product-compliance
Lightning Source LLC
Chambersburg PA
CBHW071144220526
45467CB00015B/1899